APJ Abdul Kalam —The Missile Man of India

Dr. APJ Abdul Kalam is one of the most distinguished scientist of India. He is a renowned professor, aeronautical engineer and the chancellor of the Indian Institute of Space Science and Technology (IIST).

Dr. APJ Abdul Kalam served as the 11th President of India from 2002 to 2007. He is often referred as 'People's President'. He is also popularly known as the 'Missile Man of India', because of his extraordinary contribution in the development of Ballistic Missile project and Space Rocket Technology. He also worked as a scientist in ISRO and DRDO. He was awarded with the Bharat Ratna—India's highest civilian honour in 1997.

Birth and Early Years of Dr. Kalam's Life

Dr. APJ Abdul Kalam was born in Rameshwaram (in Tamilnadu) in a middle-class Muslim family on 15th October 1931. His father was Jainulabdeen and mother was Ashiamma. Dr. Kalam's full name is Avul Pakir Jainulabdeen. His father was a devout Muslim, who had good relations with the Rameshwaram temple priests. He used to rent his owned boats out to the local fishermen. He was a good friend of the Hindu religious leaders and school teachers of Rameshwaram.

During his childhood, Dr. Kalam lived very close to the sea. He developed a great passion for nature and sea. He used to spend a lot of time watching the waves of sea. His mother influenced him to a great extent in developing his talents in music and writing poetry.

Dr. Kalam's parents led a very simple lifestyle. They imbibed good moral values in their children. Dr. Kalam became religious at a very young age. He reads 'Quran' and 'Bhagwat Geeta' daily and strictly follows vegetarian diet. Dr. Kalam devoted his entire life in doing research work.

Dr. Kalam spent most of his childhood in financial problems. His education began in a rural primary school at Rameshwaram. Later, he was shifted to Ramnathpuram Missionary School.

Dr. Kalam started working at a very early age. To bear the expenses of his education, he worked as a newspaper hawker.

His teachers, parents and others noticed his efforts and brilliance. Some of his teachers even came forward to help him.

After completing his school education in 1954, he took his graduation degree in Physics from St. Joseph College, Tiruchirapalli. In 1957, Kalam completed Bachelor of Engg. in Aerospace engineering from Madras Institute of Technology. Later he obtained advanced master and doctorate degrees in his respected field from the same institute.

Dr. Kalam's Professional Life

After completing his third year at MIT, he joined Hindustan Aeronautics Limited (HAL), Bangalore as a trainee and worked on the piston and turbine engines. In 1958, he came out of Hindustan Aeronautics Limited as a graduate.

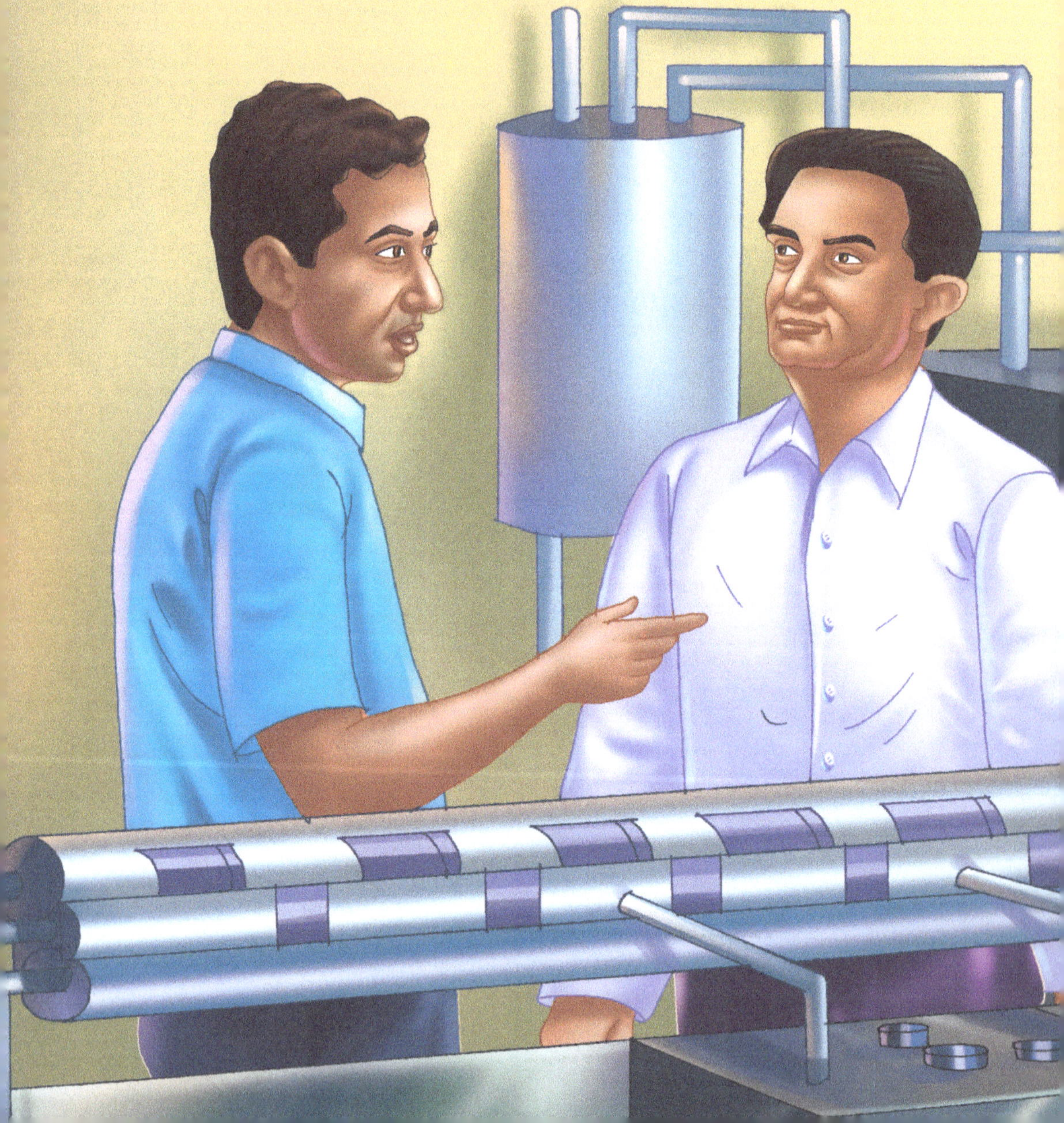

Thereafter, he got the opportunity to sewed at Indian Space Research Organisation (ISRO). After working on the several projects, he soon became a Project Director for India's first indigenous satellite launch vehicle (SLV-III) at Thumba.

The SLV-3 project was successful in placing Rohini—a scientific satellite—into orbit in July 1980 and was honoured with a Padma Bhushan in 1981. During this time, Dr. Kalam got to work with three great minds—Dr. Vikram Sarabhai, Professor Satish Dhawan and Dr. Brahm Prakash. He has also acknowledged these three people in his autobiography.

The second phase of Dr. Kalam's professional life started when he joined Defence Research Development Organisation (DRDO) in 1982. As Director of DRDO, he was entrusted with Integrated Guided Missile Development Program (IGMDP).

He played a major role in the development of many important Missiles like Nag, Akash, Trishul, Agni and Prithvi.

Three new laboratories for missile technologies were also developed during his tenure. His contributions in India's defence system are admirable.

Thereafter, Dr. Kalam worked as the Chairman of the Technology, Information, Forecasting and Assessment Council (TIFAC).

Dr. Kalam played a significant role in India's Pokharan-II nuclear test that was conducted in 1998.

In November 1999, Dr. Kalam was appointed as the Chief Scientific Advisor to the Govt. of India.
Later, in November 2001 he Joined Anna University at Chennai as a Professor of Technology and Societal Transformation.

Dr. Kalam—A Great Leader

When Dr. Kalam was working at the Rocket launching station in Thumba, there were around 70 scientists working under his leadership. To get success in their work and plan the scientists used to work for 12 to 18 hours daily. They could hardly spare any time for their families.

One day, a scientist came to Dr. Kalam and said, "Sir, I've promised my kids to take them to the exhibition going on in the town. So, I want to leave at 5.30 pm today, if you permit."

Dr. Kalam accepted his request and permitted him to leave at 5.30 pm. The scientist got engaged in his work. But when he finished the work it was almost 8.00 pm. He felt very bad that he had broken the promise given to his kids. Dr. Kalam was not in the office at that time.

In a Sad and tired mood, when he reached home he saw that his children were not at home. He asked to his wife about them. She replied, "Your Boss came here around 5.00 pm and took our kids for the exhibition."

The scientist was overwhelmed by the sweet gesture of his boss. Actually, Dr. Kalam saw that the scientist was engrossed in a very important work. And, he didn't want to disappoint the kids. So, he decided to take his children on his behalf for the exhibition.
Such an understanding and caring boss was Dr. Kalam.

Dr. Kalam as the President of India

The entire nation was surprised when the ruling NDA Government nominated Dr. Kalam—the famous scientist—as their candidate for the President elections. He won the election by huge margin and became the 11th President of India on 25th July 2002.

In his speech during the oath taking ceremony, Dr. Kalam said that we should be proud of our country, "In the last 50 years, India has made many achievements in the fields of food production, health sector, higher education, media & mass communication, information technology, science and defence. In spite of these advancements, a large population is still struggling with the problems like poverty, unemployment, diseases and lack of education."

Dr. Kalam expressed his vision to eradicate all the problems from the country and making it the strongest nation one day.

During his tenure, Dr. Kalam worked especially in the fields of science and education. He was remained as an approachable and humble President. He is very fond of the children and is always concerned for their development and welfare. He aimed to make India a scientifically strong nation and always tries to ignite the spark in the minds of Indian citizens.

Dr. Kalam has a multifaceted personality. Apart from being a great scientist, he is also interested in the field of arts and culture. He has written many books including his autobiography, 'Wings of Fire'. Some of his famous books are: 'Scientist to President', 'Ignited Minds: Unleashing the Power Within India', 'India 2020' etc.

He has also written Tamil poetry. Dr. Kalam is good at playing the Indian musical instrument 'Veena'.

Dr. Kalam has three visions. His first vision is freedom. He said that our country was ruled by many and remained dependent for a long period but we the Indians respect other's freedom, thus India has great values and culture.

Dr. Kalam's second vision is development. He said that though we have achieved a lot in the last few years, but we need to have more development, especially in the fields of education, science and technology.

His third vision is that India must be strong and emerge as a super power. It should stand up to the world and show its strength.

Dr. Kalam wants to make India an advanced and technologically developed nation. In his book, 'India 2020', he has mentioned an action plan to make India a knowledge superpower and a developed nation by the year 2020.

Dr. Kalam has been awarded with Bharat Ratna (1997), Padma Vibhushan (1990), Padma Bhushan (1981) and also received many more prestigious honours and awards.

He is presently the Chancellor of the Indian Institute of Space and Technology and also works as a professor at Anna University (Chennai) and as a visiting faculty in many academic and research institutes through out the country.

In May 2011, Dr. Kalam started a new mission for the Indian youth. 'What Can I Give Movement', is a unique mission to inculcate the Universal spirit of giving in the youth.

For years, Dr. Kalam has been inspiring many lives, especially the youth and children. He is the ocean of knowledge. We should draw inspiration from his life and must work to make India- a strongest nation.

On July 27, 2015, Dr. Kalam died after collapsing, while delivering a lecture at IIM, Shillong, Meghalaya. He was 83. The whole Nation mourned on his death, and paid homage, includes the President, the PM and other dignitaries, to him.

Chatrapati Shivaji Maharaj
—The Great Indian Warrior

Chatrapati Shivaji Maharaj was a legendary warrior of India. He was a Maratha aristocrat of 'Bhosle' clan who founded the Maratha Empire.

Chatrapati Shivaji also founded an independent Hindu kingdom, 'Hindavi Swarajya'. He inspired and united the common man to fight against the tyranny of Mughal ruler, Aurangjeb.

Chatrapati Shivaji had extraordinary military skills. His original name was Shivaji Bhosle. He was given the title of 'Chatrapati' (sovereign) by his people, for his great capability to protect them. He has been a source of inspiration for all the generations.

Birth and Early Years of Shivaji's Life

Shivaji was born on 19th February 1630, in the hill-fort of Shivneri in the Junnar city of Maharashtra. His father Shahji Bhosle was the leader of a band of mercenaries who served the Deccan Sultanates. His mother was Jijabai, the daughter of Lakhujirao Jadhav of Sindkhed.

Before Shivaji's birth, his mother Jijabai prayed to the local deity 'Shiva Bai' to bless her child with great skills. Shivaji was named after the deity.

Shivaji shared a very special bond with his mother. He was extremely devoted to her. She was a religious woman. Being in a religious environment with his mother, Shivaji also became highly religious. He read two great Hindu scriptures— the Ramayana and the Mahabharata.

रामायण

These two scriptures made a strong impression on Shivaji's young mind. Since childhood, he was highly inclined towards Hinduism and its dignity.

During the time of Shivaji's birth, Deccan was ruled by three Islamic sultanates—Bijapur, Ahmednagar and Golkunda. Shivaji's father lived mainly in Banglore but he

kept Jijabai and Shivaji in Poona. Jijabai's father deputed a master named Gomaji Naik Pansambal to take care of her and Shivaji.

Gomaji Naik remained with Shivaji throughout his life and played a very important role in his life. He helped Shivaji to become very strong. He gave him the training in horse riding, war skills and use of weapons. He also taught swordsmanship to Shivaji.

When Shivaji was 12-year old, he was taken to Banglore, where he received the formal training. At the age of 14, he returned to Poona with rajmudra (sovereign seal) and the council of ministers.

Shivaji was also trained by some Maratha warriors like Baji Pasalkar. He became a skilled warrior, horseman and strategist at a very young age.

Shivaji made a team of his trusted comrades and soldiers, who were mainly from the Maval region. With his team, Shivaji wandered in the hills and forests of Sahyadri region to collect information about the land.

In 1639, Shivaji led a large army of comrades, soldiers and officers.

At the age of 17, Shivaji decided to fight the sultanates. He, along with his friends, took a formal oath to free the country from the clutches of Muslim tyranny. This oath taking ceremony took place in a Lord Shiva temple in Rajreshwar. Shivaji was inspired and supported by his mother Jijabai for taking this oath.

Confrontations and Battles of Shivaji

In the year 1645, at the young age of 16, Shivaji was ready to fight his first battle against the Sultanate of Bijapur. His first military action was attacking and capturing of the Torna Fort, which was under Bijapur sultanate.

In 1647, Shivaji attacked and captured Kondana and Raigad forts. He also got the control of most of the southern region of Poona.

In 1654, Shivaji captured the forts of Western Ghats and also the Konkan coast. In 1648-49, Adilshah imprisoned Shivaji's father. He sent an army to fight with Shivaji. Adilshah also sent an army to fight against Shivaji's brother Sambhaji at Banglore.

Both the armies of Adilshah were defeated by the Bhosle brothers. Shivaji then gained the confidence of the Mughals, who forced Adilshah to release Shivaji's father.

Adilshah then sent Afzal Khan, an experienced general to defeat Shivaji. Afzal Khan destroyed Hindu temples at Tuliapur and Pandharpur. Shivaji decided to meet Afzal Khan for negotiations. The two met at the foothills of Pratapgarh fort on 10th November 1659.

It is said that during this time, Shivaji had a vision of Goddess Bhavani. She showered her blessings on him and promised Shivaji's victory.

Before going for the meeting, Shivaji hid some weapons under his clothing and wore an armour. As custom, they embraced each other but Afzal Khan stabbed Shivaji in his back.

Shivaji's armour protected him and he survived the attack. Shivaji then counter attacked Afzal Khan with his weapons. Afzal Khan stumbled on his knees. Collapsing into a palanquin, Afzal Khan fell down. He was slain before he could do anything.

Two of the Afzal Khan's attendants attacked Shivaji. But Shivaji and Jiva Mahal (Shivaji's bodyguard) defeated them also.

After slaying Afzal Khan, Shivaji moved towards the Pratapgarh fort with his army. Shivaji's army attacked Afzal Khan's forces.

In 1666, Aurangzeb invited Shivaji and his elder son to Agra and then he imprisoned them. Shivaji made a brilliant plan to escape. He feigned a fatal sickness in the prison. He got the permission to send shipments of offerings to priests, fakirs etc., to pray for his recovery.

One day, Shivaji and his son dressed like saints hid themselves in the boxes that were to be sent as offerings. In this way, they escaped from the prison of Agra.

The most important battles and clashes of Shivaji's life were: Battle of Pratapgarh, Fall of Bijapur Army, Battle of Kolhapur, Seige of Panhala, Battle of Vishalgarh, Clash with Mughals, Battle of Umberkhind, Fight with Shaista Khan, Clash with Aurangzeb at Agra, Battle of Nesari, etc.

Shivaji's Coronation and Rule

In June 1674, Shivaji was coronated as the king of Marathas. Under his mighty rule, the small independent land, 'Hindavi Swarajya' became a large kingdom. Hindavi Swarajya ranged from the Northwest India to the East.

Shivaji's coronation ceremony was organised in a grand manner in the Raigad fort. Thousands of people attended the ceremony. Many priests from all over came to conduct the rituals and crown the Maratha king—Chatrapati Shivaji.

After a few days of Shivaji's coronation, his mother Jijabai passed away. It was the most depressing period for Shivaji, as he was highly attached to his mother.

After sitting on the throne, Shivaji attacked and captured many places in South, like Khandesh, Phonda, Karwar, Kolhapur, Athni, Belgaum, etc.

Shivaji was a mighty ruler. His administration was also admirable. He established an able government and introduced the concepts like cabinet, foreign affairs and internal intelligence.

Shivaji had strong military powers. His military skills are compared to that of Napoleon. He used the advanced guerilla warfare tactics and intelligent networks during his battles. Shivaji also established a navy.

Shivaji had a strong bond with his people. He welcomed the people of all the sections of society to his court. He brought revolutionary changes in the welfare of the society.

By the end of Shivaji's life, he had the control of about 360 forts. He also built some new forts like Sindhudurg fort.

Shivaji was well versed in Sanskrit and Marathi languages. He had many great Sanskrit scholars and poets in his court. He promoted the use and development of Sanskrit language to a great extent.

Shivaji tried to eradicate many social issues of that time. He ended slavery in his kingdom. He also worked for the welfare and rights of women. He was successful in improving the status of women in the society.

Shivaji had eight queens. He had two sons and six daughters.

Last Years of Shivaji's Life

In the last years of Shivaji's life, his health deteriorated drastically. After a prolonged sickness, the great Maratha king breathed his last in April 1680.

After his death, his eldest son Sambhaji sat on his throne. Shivaji is remembered and revered for his struggle against imperial powers. He became an Indian icon. Many Indian warriors and freedom fighters were inspired by his bravery and courage.

Many significant public buildings were renamed on Shivaji's name. The most important of these are Mumbai's Chatrapati Shivaji International Airport and Chatrapati Shivaji Terminus.

Shivaji has been a source of inspiration for many authors, writers, artists, poets and film directors. There are many books written on the life of Shivaji. Some movies and TV serials are also made on his heroic life.

Swami Vivekananda once said, "Shivaji is one of the greatest national saviours who emancipated our society and our Dharma when they were faced with the threat of total destruction. He was a peerless hero, a pious and God-fearing king and verily a manifestation of all the virtues of a born leader of men described in our ancient scriptures. He also embodied the deathless spirit of our land and stood as the light of hope for our future."

Shivaji's birthday, 19th February, is celebrated as 'Shivaji Jayanti' in India.

Chatrapati Shivaji taught Indians to fight for their rights and face the difficult situations with courage. We can learn a lot from Shivaji's life. His unique qualities should be inculcated to lead successful and memorable lives.

Chatrapati Shivaji Maharaj will always be remembered as a great hero of Indian history.